Did You Ever Wonder about
Things You Find in the Woods?

written and illustrated by Vera Vullo Capogna

BENCHMARK BOOKS

MARSHALL CAVENDISH

NEW YORK

Benchmark Books
Marshall Cavendish Corporation
99 White Plains Road
Tarrytown, New York 10591-9001

Library of Congress Cataloging-in-Publication Data
Capogna, Vera Vullo
Did you ever wonder about things you find in the woods? / Vera Vullo Capogna.
p.   cm. — (Did you ever wonder?)
Includes index.
Summary: Describes various plants and animals that can be found in the woods,
including wildflowers, trees, birds, and reptiles.
ISBN 0-7614-0852-5   (lib.bdg.)
1. Forest animals—Juvenile literature. 2. Forest plants—Juvenile literature.
[1. Forest animals. 2. Forest plants.] I. Title. II. Title: Did you ever wonder about
things you find in the woods? III. Series.
QL 112.V85   1999   578.73—dc21   99—32140   CIP   AC

Printed in Hong Kong
1 3 5 6 4 2

This book is dedicated to my family—
to my parents, Jack and Lillian; my sisters, Roe and Johnna;
my children, Nicole, Michael, and Brandon;
and, especially, to my husband, Bob

With thanks, also, to Alison Tews and the people at the South Shore Nature Center, East Islip, New York, for their help. And to James A. Ebert, wildlife biologist at the Fire Island National Seashore, Long Island, New York, for his generous assistance.

Life in the woods changes with the seasons.

In the winter the woods are quiet and still. Many animals sleep the cold months away in their burrows or dens. Most of the birds are gone, having left in search of warmer weather.

The woods come to life in the spring. Tree buds open. Pretty wildflowers bloom. Birds return and sing out loud. Woodpeckers hammer on tree trunks.

Then summer arrives. Animals rest quietly in the summer heat. Box turtles bury themselves in the shade under leaves. Chipmunks stay in their cool burrows. Frogs lie still in the mud of the pond.

Autumn brings cooler weather. Leaves turn beautiful shades of red, yellow, and orange and begin to drop from the trees. Squirrels scurry about in search of nuts to store for the coming winter.

Have you ever walked through the woods and listened to the hammering of woodpeckers? Did you ever wonder why they peck? Did you ever wonder what woodland animals eat? Or how plants and flowers grow in the darkness of the woods?

The woodlands are a curious place. Read on to find out about all the things you may see while walking through the woods.

The woods are filled with trees. Did you ever notice how many different kinds of trees there are?

If you visit the woods in the winter, you will notice that the branches of many trees are bare. They lost their leaves in the autumn. New leaves will grow on these trees in the spring.

Some trees never lose their leaves and are always green. That is why they are called evergreens. You can recognize these trees by their odd leaves, which are actually little green needles.

You can find cones growing on evergreen trees. They contain the trees' seeds.

Trees can be told apart by their leaves. Every kind of tree grows a differently shaped leaf.

Another way to tell trees apart is by their flowers and fruit.

Trees can also be identified by the color and texture of their bark.

MAPLE

Maple trees can be recognized by their winged seeds (often called poly-noses).

In autumn maple leaves turn bright red, yellow, and orange.

Maple leaves grow in pairs.

maple seeds

OAK

Oak trees can easily be recognized by their acorns. You'll find them scattered on the woodland floor beneath these trees.

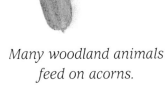

Many woodland animals feed on acorns.

BIRCH

One way to recognize a birch tree is by its bark. Thin layers of bark peel from the trunks of most birch trees.

The leaves of birch trees are oval and have toothed edges.

Wherever there are trees, there are birds. Woodland birds need trees for food and shelter.

While in the woods, you are likely to see a woodpecker. If you don't see one, you probably will hear one. Woodpeckers peck on trees for several reasons. One reason is to search for food. They climb up tree trunks, pecking with their pointy beaks. Then they eat insects that are hiding in the bark.

Another reason woodpeckers peck is to dig out holes in tree trunks. They lay their eggs in these holes.

Male and female woodpeckers also peck as a way of talking to each other.

HAIRY WOODPECKER

The tail feathers of a woodpecker are stiff and pointy. They help the bird steady itself as it climbs.

Another bird you may see in the woods is a nuthatch. You'll probably spot it climbing down a tree trunk headfirst.

The nuthatch feeds very much like a woodpecker. It even has a bill shaped like a woodpecker's bill. But unlike a woodpecker, this bird travels *down* tree trunks, not up. In this way the nuthatch finds insects that the woodpecker may have missed on its way up!

RED-BREASTED NUTHATCH

TUFTED TITMOUSE

BLACK-CAPPED CHICKADEE

If you see a small bird flying from branch to branch, it may be a titmouse. Titmice and their relatives, the chickadees, are very active and noisy birds. Sometimes you'll see them hanging upside down from tree branches in search of insects to eat.

Both of these birds will come quite close to people. They may even grab a sunflower seed from an outstretched hand.

Along with birds, many other animals make the woods their home.

While walking along, you may see or hear a deer running away. Deer are shy animals. They quickly run for cover at the sight or sound of people.

White-tailed deer are common in many woodlands. They are named for the white patch of fur under their tails. As they run from danger, they lift their tails straight up in the air, showing the white patch. This white spot is a warning signal to other deer. It lets them know danger is near.

Deer feed on the leaves of low tree branches. They also eat grass, twigs, and bark.

Fawns are born with white spots that help camouflage them in the woodlands. The spots disappear as they grow.

You'll definitely see squirrels in the woods. Tree squirrels usually make their homes in hollow tree trunks. Sometimes they build nests in tree branches.

A small relative of the squirrel, the chipmunk, lives in the woods, too. Chipmunks stay closer to the ground than squirrels do. They use low bushes and plants for food and for hiding places. They live underground in burrows where they spend the winter.

Chipmunks carry food back to their burrows in cheek pouches.

Chipmunks are not as shy as most other woodland animals.

You may find a box turtle living in the woods. During the summer box turtles bury themselves under logs or leaves to stay cool. If you visit the woods after a summer rain shower, you may see them among the puddles. They are looking for any earthworms that may have been washed out of their burrows.

When box turtles are frightened, their top and bottom shells close up tightly, like a box. That is how they got their name.

A box turtle's shell closes up completely, protecting its whole body.

Nighttime in the woods brings out some animals that you might not see during the day. Many woodland animals, such as the raccoon, sleep during the day and become active at night.

Raccoons spend the day high up inside hollow trees, where they are safe from enemies. At night they climb down to search for food.

Since raccoons are both good climbers and good swimmers, they can reach many different kinds of food. They may eat birds' eggs from a nest in a tree. Or fish from a nearby pond. Or berries, nuts, worms, insects, crabs, snails, frogs, or mice. Raccoons eat almost anything! They are also known for their unwelcome visits to nearby houses in search of garbage.

A raccoon's front paws have five fingers, just like a person's hands. This makes it easy for them to lift the lids of trash cans.

Rabbits make tasty meals for many woodland animals. For this reason they hide during the day. They come out at dusk to nibble on grass, bark, and twigs.

There are other ways that rabbits protect themselves. A rabbit's long ears allow it to hear very well. With its large eyes on each side of its head, a rabbit can see in different directions at once.

Long hind legs make these animals fast runners. A rabbit sometimes tricks its chaser by stopping short, then quickly changing direction. Rabbits escape from many enemies this way.

The cottontail rabbit got its name because its tail looks like a cotton ball.

Rabbits sometimes sit perfectly still, hoping not to be seen. Since they blend in with their surroundings, they are hard for an enemy to spot.

COTTONTAIL RABBIT

Another woodland animal that comes out at night is the owl. Owls are great hunting birds. They fly through the woods at night hunting for small mammals such as squirrels and rabbits.

One reason owls are such good hunters is that they can see well in the dark. Their large eyes allow them to spot their prey in very little light.

Owls also have soft, fluffy feathers, which help them fly very quietly. Without the noise of flapping wings, owls are able to hear faint sounds made by their prey. The owl can then swoop down silently on its victim.

GREAT HORNED OWL

During the day owls sit still on tree branches, where they blend in with the bark.

Bats are the only mammals that can fly.

Insect-eating bats have long ears that help them find their way in the dark.

Many kinds of bats fly at night, looking for insects to eat. These bats use their ears, not their eyes, to find their way in the dark.

As a bat flies, it sends out sounds from its nose or mouth. These sounds bounce off objects that might be in the bat's way. By listening to the sound waves as they bounce back, the bat can tell where the objects are. Bats also locate insects in this manner.

Many people are afraid of bats. Bats are actually shy creatures that are more helpful than harmful. They eat annoying insects such as mosquitoes. One bat can eat more than five hundred insects in one night!

During the day woodland bats sleep in trees, hanging upside down from the branches.

Many different kinds of plants grow in the woods.

Poison ivy is a plant that you probably have been warned not to touch. To follow that advice, you will need to know what the plant looks like.

The leaves of the poison ivy plant always grow in groups of three. Small whitish flowers grow in clusters on the plant. In the fall the leaves turn red, and white berries appear.

All parts of the poison ivy plant contain a poisonous sap. If you touch poison ivy, a very itchy rash will appear on your skin.

Poison ivy can be found climbing up a tree or growing along the ground.

Have you ever noticed that many woodland trees are covered with patches of green? You may be surprised to learn that these green patches are actually tiny plants growing close together. These plants are called moss. Each tiny moss plant has its own stem and leaves.

Mosses do not need dirt in order to grow. They are not like other plants, which suck up water from the soil. Instead, mosses absorb water from the air or from moisture on their leaves and stems. That is why you can even find mosses growing on logs or rocks.

Some kinds of mosses feel soft and velvety.

Have you ever stopped to admire wildflowers in the woods?

Most woodland flowers bloom only in the spring. That is because in springtime they receive the sunshine they need to grow. In early spring, trees have not yet grown their leaves. So sunlight is able to shine through the bare tree branches and reach the woodland floor.

You may find columbine growing in rocky spots in the woods.

TRILLIUM

This pretty white trillium turns dark pink as it gets old.

During the summer, when the trees have grown their leaves, little sunlight reaches the woodland floor. Without much sunlight, it is hard for flowers to grow and bloom.

BLUEBELLS

The buds of bluebells are pink. They turn blue as they grow and open.

VIOLETS

ANEMONES

Violets were named for their color. But not all violets are this purplish color. They can be white, blue, or yellow.

Anemones are one of the first flowers to bloom in the spring. Even on the coldest spring days these flowers push their way out of the ground.

In the summer the woods are dark and moist. These are the perfect conditions for ferns and mushrooms to grow.

Ferns are featherlike plants. They do not make flowers. And they don't produce seeds. Most ferns make spores instead.

On the underside of a fern leaf there are tiny bumps. These bumps are spore sacs. Each sac contains dustlike spores. When ripe, the sacs pop open, scattering the spores in the wind. These spores may be the beginning of many new ferns.

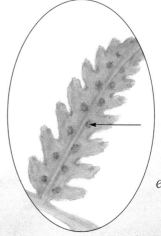

There are hundreds of spores inside each spore sac.

underside of a fern

Many different kinds of ferns grow in woodlands.

Have you ever noticed mushrooms growing in the woods? They seem to grow everywhere!

Some mushrooms grow on the woodland floor. Some grow on tree trunks. Some even grow on rotting logs.

The mushroom that you see is just a small part of the whole plant. The main part of the plant is hidden below the surface. There, tiny threads branch out far and wide in all directions. When the weather is just right, new mushrooms grow from these threads.

Mushrooms grow very fast. An overnight rain shower can cause mushrooms to pop out of the ground by morning.

Not all mushrooms are umbrella-shaped. Some are flat, with no stems, and grow from trees or logs.

Some mushrooms can be eaten, but some are poisonous. Never pick or eat a mushroom you find growing in the wild.

Waterfowl feed on plants that grow in the pond.

Quite often a walk through the woods will lead to a pond. Ponds can be found in many woodlands. Different plants and animals depend on the water in ponds to survive.

Deer can often be seen in the morning and early evening drinking from the pond. Frogs and toads lay their eggs in the water. Box turtles visit the pond now and then for a drink or to cool off in the mud.

MUTE SWANS

CANADA GOOSE

MALLARD DUCKS

female

male

Many birds build nests and raise their young near woodland ponds. Water plants and reeds make good hiding spots for their chicks.

Ducks, geese, and swans are some of the waterfowl you may see at a pond. These are large birds that have webbed feet for swimming. They have short legs and tails, but long necks. They use their long necks to look for food in and around the water.

Many kinds of turtles live in ponds, too. They find their food in or near the water. Insects, snails, water plants, and fish are all part of their diet. These turtles lay their eggs in sandy places near the water. Some woodland animals, like the raccoon, love to eat turtle eggs and often wander down to ponds in search of them.

Did you ever see several turtles resting on a log in the water? They are actually warming themselves in the sun after a swim. Sunning also gets rid of the algae and insects that feed on the turtles and harm them.

If the log is crowded, the turtles crawl on top of one another to get a spot in the sun.

You will surely see a frog near the edge of a pond. Frogs spend much of their time in water. Their webbed feet make them good swimmers.

Most frogs begin life in water. In the spring a female frog lays hundreds of eggs in the pond. Most of these eggs are eaten by fish or water insects. The ones that survive grow into tadpoles. Tadpoles are fishlike creatures. They swim underwater as fish do. As a tadpole grows, it changes into a frog.

A frog's eggs are enclosed in clear jelly balls that protect them.

About ten days after the eggs are laid, a tadpole wriggles out of the jelly ball.

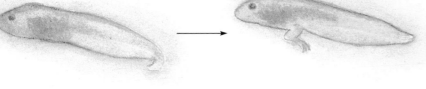

The tadpole has a long tail, which helps it swim.

At about five weeks old, it begins to grow hind legs.

In a few more weeks, front legs appear.

A few weeks later, the tadpole's tail shrinks, and its eyes get bigger.

In about fifteen weeks' time, the tadpole has turned into a frog!

The water lily is a flower you may have seen floating on the surface of a pond. Water lilies may be white, pink, or yellow.

Growing beneath the flower and its heart-shaped leaves is a long stem. Roots at the end of the stem anchor the plant to the muddy pond bottom.

The leaves of the water lily are waxy on top. Water runs off easily, allowing the plant to stay afloat.

Snails, water bugs, and small fish live among the water lilies. Larger pond creatures, such as frogs and fish, find a good supply of food there, too.

Many other kinds of plants and flowers grow in or around ponds. The cattail plant is common. Its oddly shaped flower makes it an easy plant to recognize. Long, fuzzy, and brown, the cattail flower resembles a sausage.

Cattails are found growing around the edges of ponds.

Whether it is summer or winter, spring or fall, there is always something to wonder about while walking through the woods.

GLOSSARY AND INDEX

ABSORB 19
To soak up or take in.

ALGAE 26
Tiny, simple plants that usually grow in water. Seaweeds are algae.

ANCHOR 28
To hold something firmly in place.

BARK 7, 8, 11, 15, 16
The outer covering of the trunk, branches, and roots of a tree.

BILL 9
The hard mouth of a bird.

BURROW 4, 12, 13
A hole or tunnel dug in the ground by an animal. Some animals live in burrows.

CAMOUFLAGE 11
The coloring or patterns of an animal that allow it to blend in with its surroundings. Camouflage gives an animal protection from enemies.

MAMMAL 16, 17
An animal that is warm-blooded, has a backbone, and is usually covered with fur or hair. Female mammals nurse their young.

MOISTURE 19
Water or other liquid in the air or on a surface.

POISONOUS 18, 23
Containing chemicals that can harm or kill.

POUCH 12
A pocket of skin that some animals have. Squirrels and chipmunks have pouches in their cheeks

used to carry food.

PREY 16
An animal that is hunted by another animal for food.

REED 25
A tall grass with long, thin leaves. Reeds usually grow in wet places.

ROOT 28
The part of a plant that grows down into the ground.

SPORE 22
Tiny seedlike part of some plants, from which new plants develop.

SPORE SAC 22
A small bump on some plants that contains spores.

VICTIM 16
A person or animal that is hurt or killed.

About the Author

Vera Vullo Capogna is a freelance writer and illustrator with a bachelor's degree in fine arts from the School of Visual Arts in New York City.

Inspired by her love of nature and the outdoors, she decided to write a series of nature-related books for children. Many of the topics covered in her books are in response to things her own children have wondered about.

Vera lives on Long Island, New York, with her husband and three children. She and her family have spent many pleasant hours exploring the woods near their home.